Emotional Literacy for Infant School Children

Betty K Rudd

to my children
Jase, Ben, Maria and Sophie

Lucky Duck is more than a publishing house and training agency. George Robinson and Barbara Maines founded the company in the 1980s when they worked together as a head and psychologist developing innovative strategies to support challenging students.

They have an international reputation for their work on bullying, self-esteem, emotional literacy and many other subjects of interest to the world of education.

George and Barbara have set up a regular news-spot on the website. Twice yearly these items will be printed as a newsletter. If you would like to go on the mailing list to receive this then please contact us:

e-mail newsletter@luckyduck.co.uk
website www.luckyduck.co.uk

ISBN 1 873 942 22 2

Lucky Duck Publishing Ltd
Email: publishing@luckyduck.co.uk

www.luckyduck.co.uk

Commissioning Editor: George Robinson
Designed by: Barbara Maines

Printed by Antony Rowe Limited

Contents

Worksheets - worksheets 1 to 18 inclusive may be used independently of this book as a booklet for carer and child, and this sub-section can also be offered as a colouring in book when a child is waiting to see a helper, or after a child has seen a helper.

Why is emotional literacy a good thing?

Crying and laughing are healthy! Teachers can develop in their pupils:

- the ability to feel emotions
- the opportunity to express feelings
- the capacity to be genuine
- the freedom to be honest
- an optimistic attitude
- high self-esteem.

All these qualities can be summed up by two words: emotional literacy. It has been found that emotionally literate people have reduced susceptibility to ill-health and are quicker to recover than those who are not emotionally literate (Baker, 1998). These are important reasons why emotional literacy is valuable and must not be ignored in schools. A child who is able to acknowledge and label her or his emotions tends to be a confident child (Apter, 1997).

The physical and mental aspects of individuals are linked. This has been exemplified by a study between Belgian and Dutch adults who were matched for type of work. Results showed that the Belgians suffered with more back pain than the Dutch, even though the Dutch participants had a greater work load. A striking difference was found in the mental attitude of the two groups. The group in Holland had a more positive outlook towards work, and the Belgian group was more susceptible towards depression (Baker, 1998).

It would be valuable to perform a longitudinal study of people who have been taught emotional literacy from infant school age and see whether there is a difference or not in mental attitude during adult life.

Children can also suffer from back pain. It affects nearly everyone at some time. Certain research on back pain has identified that those who "watch" their pain and try to avoid anything they think may aggravate it feel the most pain for a longer period of time (Sharon, 1998). Those who behave as normally as they can, knowing the pain is temporary, get better quicker and feel less pain (ibid.). The difference here too, is a positive attitude in the latter group (Sharon, 1998). Such an attitude can be nurtured.

Emotional attitude is connected to other health related problems such as heart attacks (Chopra, 1993). Bottled-in anger, being depressed, stressed and emotionally reserved, have all been associated with heart disease (ibid.). Indeed, people without a social network of support, who feel anxious and unhappy, have been identified as being four times more likely to die significantly younger than those who have a social support network, a positive attitude and are emotionally literate (Baker, 1998). Consequently, a key aspect of mental and physical health is emotional literacy, so it is considered paramount that teachers foster this in schoolchildren.

Expressing positive feelings and being emotionally fluid can boost the immune system (Goleman, 1996). Psycho-neuro-immunology: the investigation of the links between the mind, the immune and nervous systems, is increasingly showing the interactions between these areas and it is becoming more unrealistic to separate the mind from the body (Chopra, 1993). Although a short stressor such as giving a speech or showing a piece of work to classmates may increase immunity, long-term stress such as being bullied or the break up of a relationship, can have a detrimental effect on health (Baker, 1998). According to Baker (1998), the reason for this could be that the amount of stress hormones (for example: cortisol) being released over a long period of time, which suppress the immune system, interfere with the body's ability to protect against infection and cancer. The antidote to such stress is relaxation and being happy. It is suggested that teachers need to practice emotional literacy themselves so that they can impart it to their pupils. Perhaps they can do this by being appropriately emotionally spontaneous and taking good care of themselves, so that they can be potent positive role models for their pupils.

Laughter and tears can help prevent illness. This is because tears release stress-chemicals which have previously accumulated during a stressful time, and laughter reduces the levels of stress hormones such as cortisol while boosting an immunity antibody called immunoglobulin-A (ibid.). Incidentally, Baker (1998) says that those who are engaged in on-going cultural activities such as going to the theatre, writing, dancing or visiting art galleries, tend to live longer than people who rarely do these kinds of activities. It is not difficult to instil a love for these activities in children if their teachers enjoy them.

Feeling good and being healthy is linked to high self-esteem. If self-esteem is low, then more time is spent putting other peoples' wishes first, so there is little time and energy left to plan for health enhancing things like nutritious eating and an exercise programme. In such circumstances, it is easy to lose sight of one's individual needs and undermine one's health, while self-esteem plummets.

Children need to recognise and talk about their feelings and the photocopiable worksheets in this book can help teachers to facilitate emotional literacy in four to seven year olds. (Keystage 1) Teachers are in the favourable position of being able to make a special connection with their pupils while linking valid theory with good teaching practice. Although there is an increasing body of literature (as illustrated above) supporting the premise that a positive mental attitude improves physical well-being, what is also needed is an overall and widely available practical framework, empirically based, which guides teachers in facilitating the improvement of emotional health in every pupil.

A programme of emotional literacy within the school curriculum can give teachers a tool for working towards better class management while fostering positive behaviour in their pupils.

A teacher may the first to spot that a child is going through a change, perhaps by noticing a behavioural difference. For instance, a child may suddenly cry in the classroom. A teacher could ask this child what has brought on such behaviour. If the child will not say, the teacher may choose to respect the silence. However, if the child discloses something like: "I've got nobody to play with." this could be used in Circle Time, perhaps using the format explained by Bliss et al. (1995) so that the child is legitimately supported by other children; and an appropriate worksheet could be used (maybe one which depicts friends, such as worksheet 13). Fortunately, it is relatively easy for a network of peer support to be facilitated by teachers for their pupils. For example, each child could have perhaps a pupil who may be chronologically older, as a stress-buster-buddy to share emotions and concerns, mainly through talking. (Worksheet 4 could be introduced in such a situation).

Circle Time could also be used to develop an awareness within the children, of the importance of emotional literacy. For example, teachers could use the "sentence completion themes" suggested by Bliss et al. (1995 p. 24-27) with their pupils, as well as the worksheets in this book. These are enjoyable ways of increasing emotional awareness and literacy. Encouraging the habit of talking about troubles might protect some young people from the need for antidepressant drugs in later life.

It is hoped that eventually politicians and the media will advocate the significance of emotional health. Perhaps more can be done in society to increase a sense of worth in each individual. This could be activated by helping to raise each citizen's sense of dignity and respect by:
- raising wages for most people
- better provision for those in need
- creating jobs for the unemployed
- instilling a sense of community in the locality
- improving housing.

Eventually, society could be healthier because of robustly healthy, caring and respectful individuals.

The most effective way of being psychologically healthy is to be more expressive and aware of oneself (Gottman, 1998). Gottman states that emotionally literate children can identify their feelings, support others in distress, can concentrate well, are able to understand other peoples' points of view and have far less physical illness compared with less emotionally literate children. Maybe a fraction of the millions of pounds used to find cures for physical illnesses could be spent on investing in children; to empower them to be emotionally literate, feel worthy, have high self esteem, with a robust immune system and a positive mental attitude.

Gottman (ibid.) offers five steps in teaching emotional literacy in children, as does Goleman (1996). These are discussed in the section on how to use the worksheets.

New research

Recent research, yet unpublished, spotlights that reciprocal love and material security are what young people hope for (McGrellis et al., 1998). They fear loneliness, illness, unemployment and homelessness (ibid.). Up to date research in school-aged children highlights that these hopes and fears are common to all young people in Britain (McGrellis et al. 1998, Swallow and Romick 1998). Children need a sense of control about their future (ibid.). Currently, they feel that their sense of uncertainty depends on forces beyond their control (Nilsen, 1998). Nilsen (1998) states that they feel insecure due to a sense of danger, they feel insecure due to a sense of vulnerability and they feel insecure due to a sense of uncertainty.

Since children value relationships and fear loneliness, perhaps a new relationship can be built between the child as an individual and the school as an organisation (Martin, 1998). If more than this is needed by a pupil, then a psychological therapist can be brought into the picture. The current work of psychologists such as Makin and Ruitenbeck (1998) may help to provide new insights and value concerning relationships and aid individuals to glean what value they can when undergoing change within relationships. They advocate the importance of being in touch with one's own psychological health and doing something about it. Excitingly, teachers can propagate psychological well-being in each child who passes through their care by teaching ways of being healthy. Nevertheless, some children may also need the services of a psychological therapist.

Simons (1998), a Dutch psychologist, declares that teaching and learning are two sides of the same coin. For example, if the teacher decides the goals of learning, then their pupils cannot decide them for themselves; or if the teachers monitor learning, then their pupils will not do it for themselves. Consequently, some learning skills will not develop because practise is needed to monitor learning. Teaching can kill independent learning skills. If this has happened, then a psychological therapist may be able to facilitate independent learning in the child. Interestingly, Simons (1998) has identified how, in Finland, paradoxical tensions have been pinpointed. In particular, he argues that either the way people work together or the culture is preventing desired outcomes.

It is important to spotlight psychological wellness but, under enormous curriculum and assessment pressures, this seems to have been easy to overlook. However, the use of Circle Time in some educational establishments may have started to redress the balance.

Prevention is better than cure. Unfortunately, the cost of common mental disorders in this country is six billion pounds a year (Brown, 1998). Two-thirds of the British work-force are off work at some time in their lives, mainly due to anxiety or depression. Therefore, lack of education concerning psychological well-being results in a great cost not only to the community, but also to the individual. It is a daunting task to reduce this problem (Brown, 1998). Further, only ten per cent of these individuals are referred to specialists, since the capacity to cater for the other ninety per cent is not available. Brown (1998) argues that a great move is needed towards intervention, with the minimum of effort, to help individuals. Teachers could be key in implementing such a move.

It is suggested that if individuals were more emotionally literate, then the mental suffering, which has reached such large proportions in the UK, would be greatly reduced. Teachers are in an ideal position to teach emotional literacy, right from when children start school. This psychological approach will create a learning environment that encourages and supports good behaviour (James and Brownsword, 1998). It behoves psychological therapists to be up to date with their continuing professional development concerning emotional literacy so that they can offer courses to teachers.

It is important for psychological therapists to know that emotional literacy is considered basic for psychological well-being, (Goleman, 1996). There are certain areas to explore if a child is brought to you concerning emotional literacy. If you can involve the parents or main child-minder in your work with the child, then your job could be made easier. Lindenfield (1994) suggests looking for any of the following signs in a child:
- clinging on too long to 'babyish habits' such as thumb-sucking or bed-wetting
- underachieving at school because they are too timid to ask for help or they feel lonely
- getting over-concerned with their work and requiring it to be

too perfect
- becoming reluctant to venture from the safety of their home or town
- becoming frustratingly unable to make up their mind or give an opinion
- becoming immobilised with anxiety, fears, phobias or obsessions
- waking each night with frightening nightmares
- behaving shyly or inappropriately at social occasions
- becoming oversensitive to criticism or teasing
- developing physical symptoms of stress such as headaches, nausea or skin rashes
- showing off or bullying
- becoming persistently jealous or envious of others
- rejecting complements and giving themselves put-downs
- losing their appetite or compulsively bingeing" (p.2).

It is important to rule out Asperger's Syndrome when a child displays many of the above facets, although this disorder is not common. This can be checked against the diagnostic criteria for Asperger's Disorder from the DSM IV (1994). You can also cross-reference this with the diagnostic criteria for Asperger's Syndrome from Satmari, Bremner and Nagy (1989) and the diagnostic criteria for Asperger's Syndrome from ICD10 (World Health Organisation, 1993). The above needs to be left to psychological therapists since it is easy to become alarmed if one has only a little experience in this field.

Part three

How to use the worksheets

Teachers can teach emotional literacy by planning, implementing, assessing and record-keeping a quality curriculum for four to seven year olds. The worksheets in this publication can to be incorporated within such a framework. Psychological practitioners can integrate appropriate worksheets into whatever relevant therapeutic model they choose to use for a particular child or group. The worksheets are self explanatory and can also be used to keep young children creatively occupied while in a waiting room or whilst following up an activity. All the worksheets are photocopiable. Six key concepts encompassed by emotional literacy are covered in this section, they are:

- confidence building
- teaching how to learn
- moving towards independence
- social development
- expressing emotion
- environmental awareness.

These have been identified as essential by Mortimer (1998), an educational psychologist. All six of the above contribute to:
- A - affect (emotion),
- B - behaviour (action)
- C - cognition (thinking).

Sometimes these three qualities overlap. The use of A for affect, B for behaviour and C for cognition has been taken from the cognitive behavioural school within the field of psychology.

The foundation upon which this positive programme must be based is the communication from teacher to child of the following three qualities:
- empathy (meaning compassion),
- congruence (meaning honesty)
- unconditional positive-regard (meaning acceptance).

There is cumulative research-based and clinical evidence showing that these three qualities are necessary for movement in the desired direction (Rogers 1951, Rogers 1961, Kirscherbaum and Henderson 1989, Howe 1993, Bayne et al. 1994). A teacher interested in learning more about this work might do so by attending a foundation course on Active Listening or basic counselling skills.

The six building blocks outlined above which make up emotional literacy are incorporated within the exercises which follow and can be introduced as games. Each aspect of building emotional literacy also helps in gaining confidence. The prerequisites for confidence building are:

- feeling secure in the setting,
- learning to orientate oneself in the surroundings,
- learning the identity of other individuals,
- feeling that one belongs,
- experiencing achievement,
- having a sense of self-worth.

It is important to teach emotional literacy in a balanced way and therefore planning is essential. For instance, if you go on a journey you need to know why you are going, where your destination is and how you will get there. Why are you taking the children on this emotional literacy educational journey? Perhaps because it is fundamental that children feel confident and secure within themselves, that they learn to listen to their own needs and be respectful of others, that they learn how to learn, that they are social and healthy not only for today but also for life.

The activity sheets in this book each contribute to an emotional literacy programme. The programme is flexible so you can use your own creativity and the imagination of the children. You can use the suggested activities or adapt them so that they are tailor-made for your particular group or child.

When planning for your group or child, bear in mind the following three points:

1) Ensure that all six aspects of the emotional literacy programme or curriculum are covered. This can be done by having the list in front of you and ticking each one off as you introduce it to your group or child.
  - confidence

- learning to learn
- independence
- being social
- emotional expression
- environmental awareness.

2) Ensure that you have made provision for every child to join in - for example by copying enough worksheets.

3) Ensure that there is a link with parents and carers so they know what is going on. You can do this, for example, by either giving appropriate homework, or via a newsletter. If possible, invite parents and carers to attend a meeting about the emotional literacy curriculum. In this way they will be able to support this work at home.

Having planned the curriculum and put it into action, how do you assess it?
How much time and effort is put into emotional literacy each week?
What evidence do you have concerning the programme?

It is important to keep every scrap of evidence to support your emotional literacy programme. At an appropriate time, display all the work of your group and invite an audience so the children can show-off their personal and combined achievements. This can also be done on an individual basis. When possible, take photographs, video and audio tape recordings of individuals and groups while working on emotional literacy. (This will require informed consent from young people and their parents/carers.) The eventual bank of evidence can be extremely useful for both qualitative and quantitative research.

Record keeping in conjunction with planning must be done parallel to assessing. On the opposite page is an example of how to record progress in each part of an emotional literacy programme. It also simultaneously provides a method of assessment. This example can easily be adapted to suit your particular group's situation.

The form takes approximately a quarter of an hour to administrate. It is suggested that a record of assessment is obtained when you first have your group or child, half way through your time with the group or child, and when it is time for this group or child to move on from you. Children can also record their own personal achievements while

Child's name:

Aspects and skills	1st date:	2nd date:	3rd date:
1. Feels secure in setting			
2. Has sense of self-worth			
3. Is gaining confidence			
4. Orientates self in surroundings			
5. Respectful of others			
6. Feels she or he belongs			
7. Experiences achievement			
8. Expresses own needs and wants			
9. Listens without interrupting			
10. Is honest			
11. Has compassion			
12. Can turn-take			
13. Joins in group activity			
14. Plays with others fairly			
15. Copes with change			
16. Works alone for fifteen minutes			

with you. They can do this by implementing their own record keeping for example in the following way, and putting their worksheets in a folder (see worksheet 19).

My name is: ....

I worked on this sheet on Date:

It took me .... minutes to finish it.

I felt ....(write feeling and or draw appropriate

face) doing it.

I am *pleased,/not pleased (draw appropriate face)

.... I did it.

I know how to follow rules: Yes/No

I have a friend called ....

I feel ....

I think that

....

What I want to do is

....

The worksheets are complementary to Gottman's (1998) five principles of emotional literacy. The five aspects overarching emotional literacy which Gottman (1998) and Goleman (1996) offer as basic tenets are as follows.

   1. Knowing what emotion you are feeling in the present: this is considered as fundamental for self-awareness and insight. "People with greater certainty about their feelings are better pilots of their lives, having a surer sense of how they really feel about personal decisions from whom to marry to what job to take" (Goleman, 1996 p43).

2. Managing the emotions you are feeling. This is considered as fundamental for self-care, such as shaking off gloominess or irritability. "People who are poor in this ability are constantly battling feelings of distress, while those who excel in it bounce back far more quickly from life's setbacks and upsets" (Goleman, 1996 p43).

3. Self-motivation. This is considered fundamental for controlling your emotions and delaying gratification in order to be attentive, creative and become highly skilled. "People who have this skill tend to be more highly productive and effective in whatever they undertake."

4. Recognising the emotions others are feeling. This is considered as fundamental for empathy, and altruism, which is flamed by compassion. "People who are empathic are more attuned to ... what others need or want" (Goleman, 1996 p43).

5. Coping with relationships. This is considered fundamental for handling a relationship since much of it is concerned with managing others' emotions and underpins qualities of personal impact, leadership and popularity. "People who excel in these skills do well at anything that relies on interacting smoothly with others, they are social stars." (Goleman, 1996 pp43-44).

Some of us may be better at one skill than another, but the brain, remarkably, constantly learns, so any gaps in skills can be filled in and unremarkably, each of these five aspects "represents a body of habit and response that ... can be improved on" (Goleman, 1996 p44).

With this in mind, the following stories which are especially written with the aim of supporting four to seven year olds in their emotional literacy, can be used independently.

Stories and Activities

Jerry goes shopping (story number 1)

Jerry went shopping with his dad. He was six years old and it was two days before Nazmin's birthday party. His dad said, "Let's go to the toy shop to buy your friend Nazmin a birthday present." "Oh! Yes! Hurrah!" Jerry shouted, jumping up and down with delight. They walked up a steep hill to the zebra crossing, crossed when it was safe and went through the toy shop doorway. This shop was full of things that Jerry wanted. He looked at everything, from the little bouncy balls to the big go-carts. Meanwhile, his dad found a present which he thought would be suitable for Nazmin.

"Do you think Nazmin would like this face painting set?" he asked. "Mmmm." Jerry nodded, and carried on looking around the toy shop. In the corner of the shop he saw a lady demonstrating a bendy toy and saying, "Every child should have one." The toy fascinated Jerry, especially the way it could be bent in any position. After hearing the lady repeat her statement, "Every child should have one," he picked up a bendy toy and put it in his pocket to take home.

His father paid for the face painting set, then Jerry and his dad happily walked back to their flat holding hands. When they had arrived at their flat, Jerry's dad took the face painting set out of the shopping bag and Jerry took the bendy toy out of his pocket. "Where did you get that?" Dad shouted. Jerry looked scared. "The shop. The lady said, 'Every child should have one'", Jerry responded. "You stole it! It doesn't belong to you does it? It must go back." Jerry was very sorry that he had taken the toy and wanted to take it back to the shop. Then Jerry and his dad returned the bendy toy to the shop. Jerry cried, "I'm sorry, I won't do it again." Jerry's dad forgave him. Then they went home to wrap up Nazmin's present.

Follow-up questions and activities:

- What did Jerry do that was wrong?
- What should Jerry have done?
- What would you like for a birthday present?
- Illustrate the story.
- Make a play of the story.
- Make up a different ending for the story.

Please note that by facilitating discussions with your groups and allowing them to undergo the process of problem solving towards finding solutions to the questions and activities regarding "Jerry goes shopping", you will be aiding them in learning how to find out for themselves as well as supporting them in their social and therefore moral development.

Worksheet 20 and worksheet 5 can be appropriately used with "Jerry goes shopping".

Monique and her kitten (story number 2)

Monique was four years old and her mother brought home a gorgeous fluffy little black and white kitten during the Easter school holiday. They called it Fluffy. Monique loved Fluffy. She fed, watered and stroked it daily. One morning after breakfast, Monique wanted to play with her kitten. She called to it lovingly. She looked for it upstairs, downstairs and in the garden. She could not find it anywhere. Monique was so unhappy because she could not find Fluffy, that she started crying. Big sad tears rolled down her red little cheeks as she opened the front door.

Monique walked along the pavement outside her house crying, "Fluffy Fluffy Fluffy!" When Monique's mother noticed that the front door was open, she realised that Monique had left the house. Monique's mother rushed outside to find her. She spotted her at the corner of the pavement holding Fluffy. Quickly, she ran to bring Monique and Fluffy back into the house.

Follow-up questions and activities:

- How do you think Monique's mum felt when she saw that the front door was open?
- What do you think that Monique should have done when she could not find Fluffy?
- What do you think Monique's mother will say to her when they are back in the house?
- Act out the story.
- Make up a different ending to the story.
- Illustrate the story.

Please note that by facilitating discussions with your groups and allowing them to undergo the process of problem solving towards finding solutions to the questions and activities regarding "Monique and her kitten", you will be aiding them in learning how to find out for themselves as well as supporting them in boosting their confidence.

Worksheet 21 and worksheet 7 can be appropriately used with "Monique and her kitten".

Clever Thomas (story number 3)

Once upon a time a lovely little boy was born to two doting parents: his mother Emma and his father Aristoteles. Thomas grew to be a tall and clever seven year old. Unfortunately, he did not like going to school because some children called him "Fatty". He kept this a secret, not telling anybody, so no one knew why he did not like going to school.

One morning, Thomas would not get out of bed to go to school. When his mum and dad pulled his bed-covers off him to make him get up, he burst out crying and shouted, "I hate school! I'm never going to school!" His parents made him go. At school that day, he was very quiet and in the play ground during a play time break he picked on a small child and called him "Skinny". Then he felt guilty at being mean to the small child so he quickly said, "Sorry. I didn't mean it."

Thomas was so miserable, that he did not eat his packed lunch but only had his drink. After school, when he was at home, he went straight to his room and cried because some people had called him "Fatty" at school. That evening his mum and dad cuddled him and eventually he told them his problem.

Follow-up questions and activities:

- How do you think Thomas felt straight after he shared his problem with his mum and dad?
- What should his parents now do?
- Have you bullied any person?
- Make up the last bit of the story and finish with the words, "...and they lived happily ever after."
- Act out the story. Imagine how you would feel if you were being bullied, then draw that feeling.
- Talk about what makes you unhappy then what makes you happy.

Please note that by facilitating discussions with your groups and allowing them to undergo the process of problem solving towards finding solutions to the questions and activities regarding "Clever Thomas", you will be aiding them in learning to find out for themselves as well as supporting them in expressing their emotions and helping their social development.

Worksheet 22 and worksheet 1 can be appropriately used with "Clever Thomas".

Peter in the playground (story number 4)

There was snow in the playground and it was so cold that the children were allowed into their classrooms early. Peter was in the reception class and uncomfortable about not getting most of the attention; so he talked a lot. He did this to make others look at him. During one cold morning, the teacher told the reception class children, "All of you, during the lunch-break, stay indoors, because it is freezing cold outside". Peter was too busy talking to hear what his teacher Mr. Michael said, but all the other children heard him.

When it was lunch time, Peter put on his coat and went into the playground. Nobody else was there, and his fingers were so cold that he found it hard to move them. A dinner lady found him shivering, huddled in a corner of the playground. "Why aren't you in your classroom?" she said. "We're not allowed in during lunch time". Peter explained. The dinner lady responded, "I know, but today your teacher said that you are allowed in. I'll take you to your teacher." When Peter was taken to his teacher, Mr. Michael explained why it was important for him to stop talking and listen sometimes.

Follow-up questions and activities:

- When should have Peter stopped talking to listen?
- How did Peter feel when he was alone in the playground?
- How do you keep warm?
- With a partner role play the situation for five minutes each way, One is Peter while the other finds Peter in the playground and communicates to him what he or she understands Peter's feelings to be.
- Discuss how you would feel, what you would think and do if you found Peter in the playground.
- Think of ways, on your own, of clearing the ice and snow in the playground so it is not so cold and slippery under the feet, then share what you have thought of, with your partner.

Please note that by facilitating discussions with your groups and allowing them to undergo the process of problem solving towards finding solutions to the questions and activities regarding the story "Peter in the playground", you will be aiding them in learning how to find out for themselves as well as supporting them in environmental awareness, social development, expressing emotion, moving towards independence and confidence building.

Worksheet 2 can be appropriately used with "Peter in the play-ground".

Isabella had a friend (story number 5)

It was the long school summer holiday and Isabella was going to go from the infant to the junior school in September. She had a friend called Jilly. Isabella and Jilly were playing hide-and-seek with their childminder. While Isabella was hiding, she thought, "Jilly's a long time finding me. I wonder if she's stopped looking for me? I'll go and find her and my childminder." Neither Isabella nor her childminder could find Jilly.

Eventually, they heard her shouting, "Look what Isabella's done to the car!" Isabella did not know what Jilly was talking about. Then she heard the childminder's cross voice, "Isabella! You naughty girl! I don't like having you here if that's the kind of thing you're going to do! I'm telling your granny!" (Isabella lived with her grandmother.) Isabella gasped, "What is it?" The childminder angrily pulled Isabella to her car which was parked in the garage. The word "Isabella" had recently been scratched onto it, in secret, by Jilly. Isabella said, "I didn't do it". Jilly looked at the childminder, straight into her eyes, and clearly said, "Yes she did". The childminder did not know whether to believe Jilly. Nevertheless, she telephoned Isabella's grandmother so that Isabella could be taken home early that day. The childminder also made arrangements for Jilly to go home early too. While waiting for her granny, Isabella insisted to the childminder that she did not scratch the car. Soon, both girls were taken to their respective homes.

Follow-up questions and activities:

- What do you think should happen next in the story?
- Is there any time when you would tell a lie?
- What do you think of Jilly?
- Act out the story.
- Tell your partner of a time when someone upset you.
- Discuss ways of dealing with Jilly's lie and Isabella's feelings.

Please note that by facilitating discussions with your groups and allowing them to undergo the process of problem solving towards finding solutions to the questions and activities regarding the story "Isabella had a friend", you will be aiding them in learning how to find out for themselves as well as supporting them in social development and confidence building.

Worksheet 3 can be appropriately used with "Isabella had a friend". Further notes to use with appropriately numbered worksheets start on page 32.

Plans for Using Worksheets

Plan for using worksheet 4: Talking isn't medicine.

Aim: For children to know their emotions.

Step 1: Invite children to move how they feel while you join in.

Step 2: Invite children to make a sound describing how they feel.

Step 3: Explain how some people take medicines which can hide how they feel, and how healthy it is to know how we feel.

Step 4: Invite children to talk about how they feel.

Step 5: Handout worksheet 4 to colour in.

Plan for using worksheet 6: You can feel bad.

Aim: Managing emotions.

Ensure that all the children have access to colouring in equipment.

> Step 1: Invite children to talk about their favourite animals and pets.

> Step 2: Share a time when you had a loss and how you got over it.

> Step 3: Explain that sometimes pets do not live as long as people and how we can look after animals while they are in our care; and how we can cope with losing them, such as remembering happy memories of them.

> Step 4: Handout worksheet 6 to colour in.

Plan for using worksheet 8: You can feel bad.

Aim: Self-motivation.

Step 1: Describe a time that you felt rather distressed yet
persevered for the better, such as during a test, or not
waking up your parents at night because you knew that
there was nothing really wrong.

Step 2: Ask the children for examples of when they can
continue to do something, having a goal in mind,
for instance, saving some pocket money for an
expensive toy.

Step 3: Handout worksheet 8 to colour in.

Plan for using worksheet 9: ...you feeling good.

Aim: Identify others emotions.

Step 1: Ask children to think of two wishes, one of which is realistically possible and one impossible.

Step 2: Ask them how they can make the possible one happen.

Step 3: Show a teddy and say that teddy's wish came true.

Step 4: Say that teddy is smiling.

Step 5: Ask the children to identify teddy's emotion.

Step 6: Hand out worksheet 9 to colour in,

Plan for using worksheet 10: Five ways to feel good.

Aim: Coping with relationships.

Step 1: Show a teddy and explain that teddy is crying because his tower of bricks toppled down.

Step 2: Along comes teddy's friend dolly who cuddles teddy.

Step 3: Teddy and dolly build another tower.

Step 4: Teddy and dolly have a picnic.

Step 5: Teddy and dolly have a rest.

Step 6: Encourage the children to talk about who they like to spend their time with.

Step 7: Children brainstorm different ways of making up with a friend they have broken up with.

Step 8: Children brainstorm ways of being healthy and taking care of themselves.

Step 9: Hand out worksheet 10 to colour in.

Plan for using worksheet 11: Healthy body and mind.

Aim: Learning to learn.

Step 1: Ask children what would happen if they did not have any water for a very long time.

Step 2: Ask children what would happen if they did not eat for a very long time.

Step 3: Ask children what they feel if they do not have enough to drink.

Step 4: Ask children what they feel when they do not have enough to eat.

Step 5: Ask children what they should do when they are thirsty.

Step 6: Ask children what they should do when they are hungry.

Step 7: Handout worksheet 11 to colour in.

Plan for using worksheet 12: Grow strong and healthy.

Aim: Independence.

Step 1: Draw a seed.

Step 2: Draw roots on the seed.

Step 3: Make the above into a seedling.

Step 4: Change the seedling into a flower.

Step 5: Think of what was needed so that the seed could grow into a strong and healthy flower.

Step 6: Think about what you need to grow strong and healthy.

Step 7: Colour in worksheet 12.

Plan for using worksheet 13: Play with friends.

Aim: Being social.

Step 1: In a circle, helper whispers either "duck", "cow" or "pig" to each child.

Step 2: With eyes closed, children make either "quack", "moo" or "oink" sounds, moving around until they are in three groups, a group of ducks, one of cows and another of pigs.

Step 3: Each group make up a play lasting about two minutes, about a visitor who comes to stay in our world from a different world, so the guest needs to be taught how to be polite and well-mannered.

Step 4: Each group shows their mini-play to the other groups.

Step 5: Hand out worksheet 13 to colour in.

Plan for using worksheet 14:   Grow and heal.

Aim: Environmental awareness.

Step 1: Think about a dirty and untidy room.

Step 2: Talk about how to make it clean and tidy.

Step 4: Discuss the importance of caring for our environment.

Step 5: Think about getting enough sleep and why we need it.

Step 6: Draw a picture of what you think that you would like
to do if you were feeling tired after working hard at
cleaning and tidying up.

Step 7: Colour in worksheet 14.

Plan for using worksheet 15: Be happy.

Aim: Happiness.

Step 1: Talk about the importance of feeling fine about yourself so you can be happy.

Step 2: With a partner, think of all the things that make you happy.

Step 3: In groups, write and draw all the things that make you happy.

Step 4: Each group share what makes them happy.

Step 5: Each child decides what they will do to be happy.

Step 6: Colour in worksheet 15.

Plan for using worksheet 16: Your feelings.

Aim: Express feelings.

Rule: Do not touch anyone or anything and stay in your "corner" while shouting.

This is called "the three cornered game or exercise" and the helper can demonstrate it first.

Step 1: Three children stand at three points of an invisible triangle. One corner is called "the love corner", the other is called " the need corner" and the third is called "the hate corner".

Step 2: At a given signal the three children simultaneously shout "I love you", "I need you" and "I hate you", respectively for about ten seconds. Then in a clockwise direction they change places, then after another ten seconds of shouting their different word they change places again, so after approximately thirty seconds, each child has had a turn expressing need, hate and love.

Step 3: Do this until all children have had a turn.

Step 4: Discuss how each child felt doing the above and say that this is a warm up used by some actors, since they need to be able to express emotions.

Step 5: Handout worksheet 16 to colour in.

Plan for using worksheet 17: Balance your life.

Aim: To gain confidence.

Rule: Freeze at a given signal and continue at another given signal.

The above rule may need to be practised a few times before the following game/exercise begins.

Step 1: The children each simultaneously mime what they do from getting up in the morning to sleeping at night.

Step 2: At various times throughout the miming, ask the children to freeze in their positions apart from one or two children, whom the rest watch for a few moments, before all continue with their mimes again.

Step 3: As in step 2 until all the children have had the opportunity to individually show some of their mime to the others.

Step 4: Discuss the importance of a balanced life. For example, if you do not eat anything except sweets you will get too fat, develop spots and lose some teeth.

Step 5: Hand out worksheet 17 to colour in.

Plan for using worksheet 18: Be kind to yourself.

Aim: Keep sight of your own needs.

Rule: In the following game/exercise, when pretending to be a sleeping lion, you are not allowed to move or make a sound (remember to breathe).

Step 1: Find a space and pretend to be a sleeping lion.

Step 2: Listen to sounds outside the building you are in.

Step 3: Listen to sounds outside the room you are in.

Step 4: Listen to sounds inside the room you are in.

Step 5: Listen to yourself, such as your breathing and heartbeat.

Step 6: Think of all that you need to keep yourself happy and healthy and imagine giving yourself all that you need whenever you need it.

Step 7: Colour in worksheet 18.

Plan for using worksheet 23: Feel secure in setting.

Aim: For children to feel secure in their setting.

Ensure that the toilet is clean before starting this activity.

Step 1: Escort your group of children on a guided tour around the immediate vicinity showing them the following. The games area outside the room and inside the room, the work area inside and outside the room, the emotional literacy session area, the cloakroom, where the tissues are kept for runny noses, the waste paper basket, the toilet and wash basin.

Step 2: In pairs (one of the pair is named Apple and the other is Pear). Apples show Pears: a) the games, work and session areas; b) the washbasin; c) where the tissues are kept. Then the Pears show the Apples: a) the cloakroom; b) the waste paper basket; c) the toilet.

Step 3: The children stick the completed worksheet on the wall.

Plan for using worksheet 24: Sense of self-worth.

Aim: For children to have a sense of self-worth.

Step 1: The facilitator explains how each person is unique and different from the next person. For example: different colour hair, different colour skin, different shape, different size feet, different likes and so on.

Step 2: Each child is to draw her or himself. Then that child or the child's friend can colour in the hair, eyes and so on, with the appropriate colours.

Step 3: Encourage the children to share one or two pieces of information about their families. This can be done in groups where turn-taking can be practised. Comments should be kept positive.

Conclusion

If, as a teacher, your aim is to ensure that children achieve their potential, then this book supports you in fulfilling that aim. The book helps teachers facilitate a positive learning environment where each child is celebrated as she or he learns to interact fairly, learns to respect her or himself and others, learns to find things out for her or himself, learns to work as part of a team, learns to appreciate others, learns to understand her or his feelings and the feelings of others, can cope with change in a robustful way, can self-manage behaviour and also think about ways of caring for the environment.

The format for when to use the worksheets could be: at circle time, story time, or left to the discretion of the teacher. During Circle Time for example, if a child says that her or his pet has died, then the worksheet which deals with this issue could be used. The term groups is used in this book to describe children from ages four to seven years inclusive, regardless of educational attainment or number of people in a group. Groups can be in schools, hospitals, holiday clubs or elsewhere. Needless to say, psychological therapists can also make use of the worksheets as described above.

Professional helpers like teachers and psychological therapists, are faced with the needs of others, practically daily and usually for many years. In order to stay psychologically robustly healthy, the following ideas which have been extrapolated from Baker (1998) can be used as a framework for an antidote to negative stress, so the ability to handle pupils and clients does not impinge on the helpers' psychological well-being: Relax, be happy, take adequate self-care, use spontaneity, have a positive attitude, do some cultural activities (as some people who live longer do) such as going to the theatre, visiting art galleries and writing, remember the correlation between good health and feeling good, eat nutritiously, exercise regularly, keep your own needs in sight, and recognise and deal with your own feelings.

References

Apter, T., (1997) *The confident child*. Norton.

Baker, P., (1998) *Here's Health*. March 1998, 20-22.

Bayne, R., Horton, I., Merry, A. and Noyes, E. *The counsellor's handbook*. Chapman Hall.

Bliss, T., Robinson, G. and Maines, B., (1995) *Developing Circle Time* Lucky Duck Publishing.

Brown, J., (1998) Large-scale health promotion stress workshops: promotion and client response. Brighton 1998 British Psychological Society annual conference, unpublished paper.

Chopra, D., (1993) *Ageless Body Timeless Mind*. Rider.

Goleman, D., (1996) *Emotional Intelligence*. Bloomsbury.

Gottman, J., (1998) *The Heart of Parenting*. Bloomsbury.

Howe, D., (1993) *On Being a Client*. Sage.

James, F. & Brownsword, K., (1994) *A Positive Approach*. Belair Publications Limited.

Kirscherbaum, H. and Henderson, V., (1989) *The Carl Rogers Reader.* Houghton Miffin.

Lindenfield, G., (1994) *Confident Children*. Thorsons 2.

Makin, P. and Ruitenbeck D. V., (1998) The psychological contract as a close relationship. Brighton 1998 British Psychological Society annual conference, unpublished paper.

Martin, P., (1998) The psychological contract as a close relationship. Brighton 1998 British Psychological Society annual conference, unpublished paper.

McGrellis, S., Thomas, R., Holland, J. Henderson, S. and Sharpe, S., (1998) Hoping for heaven: fearing exclusion; the location of young people's fears in time and place. Brighton 1998 British Psychological Society annual conference, unpublished paper.

Mortimer, H., (1998) *Personal and Social Development*. Scholastic Limited.

Nilsen, A., (1998) The future as a nation and a point of reference in the thoughts of young people. Brighton 1998 British Psychological Society annual conference, unpublished paper.

Rogers, C., (1951) *Client-centred Therapy*. Constable.

Rogers, C., (1961) *On Becoming a Person*. Constable.

Sharon, M., (1998) *Complete Nutrition: how to live in total health*. Priori.

Simons, J., (1998) Paradoxes in learning and teaching. Brighton 1998 British Psychological Society annual conference, unpublished paper.

Swallow, B. and Romick, R., (1998) Towards the millennium: young people's values, beliefs and thoughts. Brighton 1998 British Psychological Society annual conference, unpublished paper.

Note

If you are interested in contributing to the collection of evidence for teaching emotional literacy then please send copies of your work to the author, care of the publishers. It will be understood that you agree to the contents being included in any future publication. You will be acknowledged.

Worksheets

Notes

Talking is for Kids!

Hello

I am a helper and this is

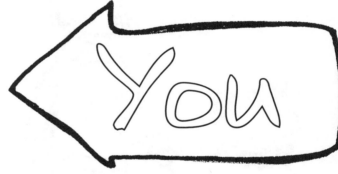

You

You have emotions, a body and a mind. Your emotions affect your body and your mind.

Talking does not use medicines.

Sometimes you can feel really bad about yourself. Talking can help you feel better about yourself.

Feeling good   Feeling bad

You can feel

bad

My dog died

if you get sad news.

You can feel **bad**

Teacher saw me copy the sums.

if you break a rule.

You can feel

bad

I heard a noise in the dark of night!

because of being scared.

This is you feeling good

This is you feeling bad

5 ways to feel good

1 Eat well.

2 Exercise lots.

3 Play hard.

4 Sleep right.

5 Be Happy.

For a healthy body and mind you need to drink water and eat good food.

You need fresh air, daylight and exercise to grow strong and healthy.

You need to play with with friends to
learn how to get on with others.

worksheet 14

You need to get enough sleep. That's when you grow and heal.

Feel good about yourself so that you can be happy.

With your helper you can safely learn to understand your feelings.

Balance your life

Spend time with others.

Rest.

Be alone sometimes.

Learn something new.

Play fair.

Be kind to your self.

The date is: **My name is**

Today I worked on:

It took me [   ] **minutes to finish it.**

I felt [   ] **doing it.**

{draw or write the feeling}

I felt [   ] **when I did it.**

{happy or sad face}

I know how to follow rules: Yes   or   No

I have a friend called [   ]

I feel [   ]

I think that [   ]

What I want to do is [   ]

Jerry goes shopping

Jerry took something that did not belong to him, so he returned it.

What do you think Jerry did that was wrong?

What does your friend think Jerry did that was wrong?

What should Jerry have done instead?

What would you like as a present?

Draw Jerry.

Monique and her kitten

Little Monique leaves her house to find her kitten.

How did Monique's mum feel when she knew Monique had left the house?

What could have Monique have done when she could not find her kitten?

What will Monique's mum say when they are back in the house?

Draw your favourite animal.

Clever Thomas

Thomas does not want to go to school because he was bullied.

Why did Thomas keep it a secret that he was being called "Fatty"?

How do you think he felt when he shared his problem?

What should happen next in the story?

Draw "Clever Thomas".

Feel secure in setting

Draw and colour in something that is outdoors:

Draw and colour in something that is indoors:

Draw an apple and colour it in:

Draw a pear and colour it in:

Write your name

Write the date

Gain sense of self-worth

My name is:

My friend's name is:

Draw your face and ask your friend to colour it in.

Don't forget to visit our website for all our latest publications, news and reviews.

www.luckyduck.co.uk

New publications every year on our specialist topics:

- ▸ **Emotional Literacy**
- ▸ **Self-esteem**
- ▸ **Bullying**
- ▸ **Positive Behaviour Management**
- ▸ **Circle Time**
- ▸ **Anger Management**
- ▸ **Asperger's Syndrome**
- ▸ **Eating Disorders**

3 Thorndale Mews, Clifton, Bristol, BS8 2HX | Tel: +44 (0) 117 973 2881 Fax: +44 (0) 117 973 1707